Therapeutic Interventions Using Non-Therapeutic Games:

BEHAVIOR BASICS FOR K-8

42 Dynamic Behavior Learning Activities for K-8 That Can Be Applied To Games You Probably Already Have In Your Closet

Paula B. Cox, Ed.S, NCSC
Farra O. Criswell, M.S. LPC

youth light inc.

© 2009, 2005
by YouthLight, Inc.
Chapin, SC 29036

Cover Design and Layout by Diane Florence
Project Editing by Susan Bowman

ISBN
1-889636-74-6

Library of Congress Number
2004110068

10 9 8 7 6 5 4 3 2
Printed in the United States

Acknowledgements

We wish to acknowledge all the children we have worked with in the past and will work with throughout our careers. Their strength and resiliency is inspiring. Also, thanks to our employers, Lee County Schools and Region III Mental Health, for allowing us the opportunity to work with children and incorporate our ideas into our work.

We would also like to acknowledge our families, who have supported us throughout this endeavor with their patience and unfailing love. And, most importantly, we would like to thank and offer praise to God for blessing us with the opportunity to see a dream become reality! Finally, we would like to thank YouthLight, Inc. for producing and promoting sound products and being a company with integrity.

About the Authors

Paula B. Cox received her B.S. degree in psychology from Blue Mountain College. She received her M.Ed. and Ed.S. degrees in counseling from the University of Mississippi. She is currently working on her Ph.D. at the University of Mississippi. Paula has worked as a Day Treatment Therapist for a community mental health center and is currently working as a School Counselor at Saltillo Elementary in Mississippi. She is a National Certified Counselor and a National Certified School Counselor.

Farra O. Criswell received her B.A. degree in psychology from Delta State University. She later received her M.S. degree in community counseling from Mississippi State University. She has worked as a case manager, a therapist at a psychiatric inpatient facility for children and adolescents, and as an outpatient therapist at a community mental health facility. She is currently working as a Licensed Professional Counselor with a community mental health center at an elementary school. She lives in Mississippi with her family.

Table of Contents

Section Six: Organizational Skills & Time Management

Section Seven: Respecting Others

Section Eight: Taking Responsibility

Section Nine: Teamwork

Appendix

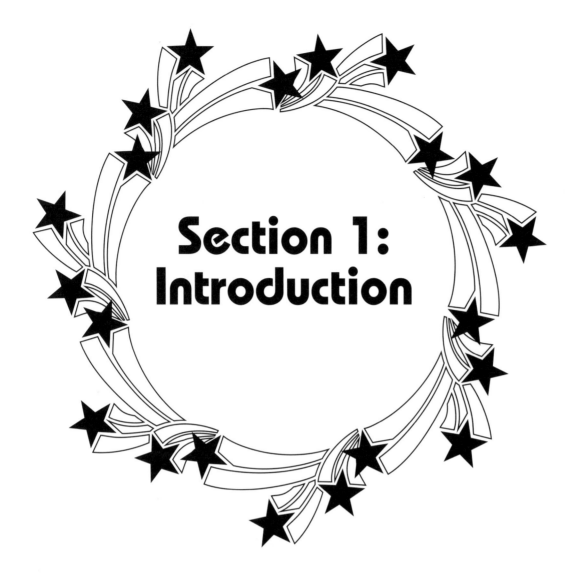

Section 1: Introduction

This section of the book provides the reader with an understanding of why this book was written and how it can be useful to the reader. Also, suggestions are included to help you utilize the activities in the book in order to best meet the needs of children who are exhibiting behaviors that fall into one of the eight categories covered.

About This Book

Necessity often breeds creativity, which was the case for us. As mental health professionals, we are constantly seeking innovative, yet practical ideas for sessions. *Therapeutic Interventions Using Non-Therapeutic Games: Behavior Basics for K-8* is such a tool. By taking recreational games, which are readily available to everyone and structuring the play of the game to a therapeutic nature, we utilized a fun and effective modality of therapy that focuses on eight behavior areas. The games needed for each session are inexpensive, and some are probably in your closet already! By using recreational games, students are already familiar with some, if not all of the games, as well as the instructions for play. The use of games provides hands-on learning, and gives the student a concrete example of the concept that is being taught. The activities are useful with children and adolescents in individual, group, or family therapies.

Anyone who is a mental health professional, school counselor, social worker, psychologist, psychiatrist, juvenile counselor, or pastoral counselor will find this book useful. Because of the easy access to the materials, these activities can be used in almost any setting such as a school, mental health facility, mental health hospital, youth detention setting, child services / welfare agencies, and private counseling offices.

By eliminating some of the more clinical discussion topics, parents can also use this book to reinforce what their child is learning in therapy. The games and activities can assist parents in teaching life skills (such as thinking before speaking) to their child in a fun, non-threatening way. Mental health professionals can use the activity covered during the session as "homework" for the family between sessions. An added bonus is that by playing these games as a family, more time will be spent together, which will hopefully strengthen the family unit.

So, grab some games and activity sheets, and get started!

Rationale

The use of recreational games in counseling is not a new idea. The therapeutic use of these games in therapy was first explored by Bettleheim (1972) using such common games as chess and poker. Crocker and Wroblewski (1975) made the case for the use of recreational games in counseling as well. The authors presented cases in which the use of non-therapeutic or recreational games such as *Risk®* and *Monopoly®* resulted in therapeutic effects for clients. However, due to today's focus on therapeutic games such as *The Self Control Game, The Anger Control Game,* etc., the value and use of recreational games in counseling seems to go unnoticed.

Recreational games provide a non-threatening means of communication and expression for the child. Oftentimes, the child is familiar with the games used in a session, and therefore, will naturally feel more at ease during the time spent with the counselor. Games also provide a means of structure, due to the rules of games and the required methods of play (Friedberg, 1996; Kottman 1990).

Friedberg (1996) suggests that in addition to games, workbooks provide therapeutic avenues in sessions with children. Workbooks and/or activity sheets can provide direction for the child and offer a concrete way of transferring ideas from the counselor's office to the classroom or at home. However, when a counselor is selecting workbooks and activities and/or games to use with a child, he or she should make sure the activities are individually tailored to meet the child's needs and not just selected randomly.

How to Use This Book

This book provides a user-friendly approach to helping children with behavior problems. Each session is outlined using a clear, concise format. A session may be selected for use based on particular behaviors and/or certain characteristics of a child. Each child and situation is unique. Therefore, it is necessary to determine that an activity is appropriate for a particular child and fits into the child's overall treatment plan.

Prior to beginning a session and/or activity, make sure you are prepared with all the necessary materials and/or games. Have copies of the follow-up activity sheets ready to be distributed to each participant.

Each session can be modified to suit your style as a counselor, parent, etc. In the discussion sections of each activity, we only intended to provide you with a guide, not an exhaustive list of questions or ideas to pursue. When a child presents something that you feel needs to be explored further, by all means, pursue the issue.

You do not have to use the name brand of the games listed in this book. If there are games that are similar in nature, just modify the activity accordingly. For example, instead of using the marketed game Hangman®, you may choose to play the game using pencil and paper.

When writing the activities for this book, we assumed that you would engage in playing the game with the child. However, exceptions to this may include times when you are working with a small group and there is limited time and/or materials, or when you do not feel this will best fit the needs of you child.

Each of the activities can be used in individual sessions or in group settings. The activities are designed for use with children in kindergarten through grades eight. Look at the heading "Grades" in each session to determine what grade levels the content is appropriate for. Please modify the activities accordingly, giving attention to the wording of particular questions and the cognition required to play the games.

Session content and activities in the book are designed for 45-60 minute sessions. However, all of the sessions can be shortened or lengthened to fit the time of the session.

A child should never be forced to participate in any of the games and/or activities. When resistance is exhibited, explore the process and/or feelings associated with the situation. Allow the resistance to be the focus of the session until the child is ready to participate and/or another issue surfaces.

If you notice a child is cheating and/or not following the rules of a game, bring this up. Re-discuss the rules and provide examples. Allow the child to discuss his or her purpose. If this continues, you may want to choose to stop the game and discuss the importance of following instructions and/or the consequences of cheating. One such consequence would be that the child is no longer allowed to play the game.

Section 2: Attending

Children often have difficulty attending (paying attention) in classroom situations and at home. In both settings, children with attention problems have difficulty listening to instructions, concentrating on tasks, and ignoring distractions. Oftentimes, these children simply lack basic skills that prevent them from being successful when trying to pay attention. Therefore, this section of the book provides five activities that are designed to increase attending skills such as memory, concentrating on tasks, listening, ignoring distractions, and concentrating in timed situations.

Do You Remember?

Objective

To provide a visual example of the importance of paying attention

Grades

K-8

Game

Memory®

Participants try to find pairs of matching cards. This game can be played with two – four people.

Directions

1. Play according to the instructions included with the game.

2. Observe the child to see if he or she is attentive when you select cards and if he or she continues to select mismatched cards that have been previously turned over.

3. Play another round, and have the child name the object on the card as he or she turns it over.

4. Offer encouragement when the child avoids selecting a card that has previously been turned over.

Discussion

1. Compare and contrast the child's success in matching pairs to the amount of or lack of attentiveness, as well as your own. Emphasize that more pairs were matched during the game when he or she was attentive. Discuss why this occurs.

2. Compare his or her success playing following direction number one versus following direction number three. What was easier and/or harder about playing each way?

3. Ask the child to identify an area at home or at school that he or she could improve in if he or she was more attentive. Identify specific examples of how being more attentive will help in that given area. Prompts may be necessary. For example, "If you knew that Ms. X was reviewing for the test on Friday, would you have taken notes? How would taking notes have helped?"

Follow-Up Activity

Provide a copy of the "Do You Remember?" worksheet on the following page for each student.

Do You Remember?

Color the pairs that match.

You were able to do this activity because you were able to pay attention. You were able to do this activity because you were able to pay attention. You were able to do this activity because you were able to pay attention. You were able to do this activity because you were able to pay attention. You were able to do this activity because you were able to pay attention You were able to do this activity because you were able to pay attention. You were able to do this activity because you were able to pay attention. You were able to do this activity because you were able to pay attention because you were able to pay attention. You were able to do this activity because you were able to pay attention. You were able to do this activity because you were able to pay attention. You were able to do this activity because you were able to pay attention. You were able to do this activity because you were able to pay attention. You were able to do this activity because you were able to pay attention. You were able to do this activity because you were able to pay attention. You were able to do this activity because you were able to pay attention. You were able to do this activity because you were able to pay attention. You were able to do this activity because you were able to pay attention.

You were able to do this activity, because you were able to pay attention!

Hocus, Pocus, Focus

Objective

To increase one's ability to concentrate on tasks instead of just making random choices

Grades

K-8

Game

Pick Up Sticks

Participants try to remove a stick without moving any of the other sticks in the pile. This game can be played by one or more people at a time.

Directions

1. Before playing, drop the sticks onto the floor/table.
   Point out how some sticks are laying on other sticks.

2. Play the game according to the instructions included with the game.

3. Offer praise when an attempt is made that required one to think prior to acting. Remember to offer encouragement even if the attempt is unsuccessful. Keep the focus on the concentration required.

Hocus, Pocus, Focus

...Continued

Discussion

1. When playing this game, what do you have to remember and/or concentrate on? As answers to the question are given, have the child point out the situations within the game. For example, a child may state that one has to remember how moving one stick will affect another stick. After he or she states the answer, have him/her point to a stick that if moved, would affect another stick.

2. Prompt the child to reach and grab a stick in the middle of the pile without thinking about it.
   - What happened when you just reached and grabbed a stick?
   - What would have prevented this from happening?

3. What do you have to remember and/or concentrate on when doing _____? (offer specific tasks/activities that are relative to the child's situation such as homework, chores, watching a movie, reading a book, etc.)
   - What are some things that you could do to help you remember to concentrate or to refocus when you get off track?

Follow-Up Activity

Provide a copy of the "Hocus, Pocus, Focus" worksheet (on the following page) for each student.

16

Hocus, Pocus, Focus

I have trouble focusing when I _____

_____.

This week, when I get off track, I can refocus by:

Look Into My Eyes

Objective

To teach good listening skills

Grades

3-8

Game

Taboo®

Teams provide verbal cues for the given word in a limited amount of time. This game requires pairs of people, so at least four people and no more than eight can play.

Directions

1. Play according to the instructions included with the game.

2. After a few attempts, stop and discuss how the game is going.

3. Play a few rounds with poor attending skills (no eye contact, fidgeting, occupying hands with an object, etc.).

4. Play a few rounds with good attending skills (eye contact, hands and body still, etc.).

Discussion

1. Discuss the differences between each method of playing. Help the child identify specific things that interfered with listening and things that helped one listen.
   - Which was more difficult for each person?
   - Which method proved more successful? Why?

2. Discuss how when playing using direction number four, one was able to keep eye contact, not fidget, etc. Guide the child into identifying specific examples as to how those same skills can be incorporated into the class room and at home.
   - Can you use those skills in the classroom? How?
   - What will be a signal in the classroom to remind you to use good attending skills?

Follow-Up Activity

Provide a copy of the "Look Into My Eyes" worksheet (on the following page) for each student.

Look Into My Eyes

Color in the places where you have trouble paying attention and/or listening.

At Home

Other Places

At School

Write under each picture how it can be used to help you pay attention.

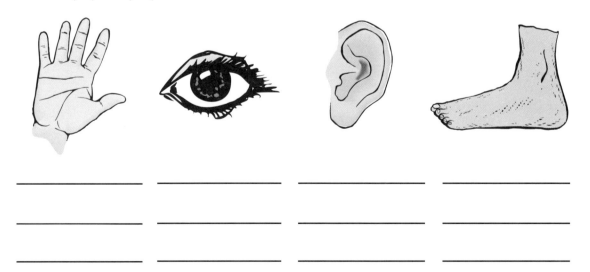

_____ _____ _____ _____

_____ _____ _____ _____

_____ _____ _____ _____

The Clock is Ticking

Objective

To practice concentration and focus in a timed situation and/or experience

Grades

K-8

Game

Bop-It® or Bop-It Extreme®

Participants quickly try to follow oral instructions given by the game. This game can be played with two or more people.

Directions

1. Prior to play, inform and discuss with the child that it is very difficult to perform tasks under pressure and/or in a timed situation.

2. Play the game according to the instructions included with the game (each person can play individually or with a predetermined amount of tries each, or each can play simultaneously with the 1 or more player option).

3. With each completion of a "round," point out positive things that the child did while playing the game.

Discussion

1. Model appropriate ways to cope with frustration and anxiety during a timed activity as you play. Explain your method of staying focused to

The Clock is Ticking
...Continued

retain the sequence. Share with the child any tips you may use while trying to remember the sequences. Ask the child to describe how he or she tries to remember the sequences. Summarize tips the child has identified that help his/her concentration.

2. Process with the child if he or she is more successful by listening only or by actually looking at the part that comes next. If he/she is unable to identify which is easier for him/her, have the child play blindfolded. Make sure he/she knows where each of the parts are that will need to be manipulated. Call out several parts prior to the child playing in order to help him/her remember where each part is located on the game.

3. Discuss the concept of how continued practice of something that is hard or anxiety provoking often helps one to perform better under those circumstances. Allow the child to practice and discuss if any progress is being made.

4. Have the child describe a situation in which he or she feels under pressure and as a result, has a difficult time performing. Refer to the tips the child identified that aided their concentration in the game, and discuss how these same tips can be applied to different situations.

Follow-Up Activity

Provide a copy of the "The Clock is Ticking" worksheet (on the following page) for each student.

22

The Clock is Ticking

Color the things that could help one concentrate and put an "X" on the things that would not help one concentrate while doing a task.

Talking on the phone

Talking to your friends

Listening closely

Sitting in a chair close to the front

Thinking about other things

Turning the lights on

 This week, I am going to try hard to concentrate more by _____.

Watching Very Closely

Objective

To assist one in developing the skill of ignoring distractions

Grades

K-8

Game

Bop-It® or Bop-It Extreme®

Participants quickly try to follow oral instructions given about the game.
This game can be used with two or more people.

Directions

1. Play according to the instructions included with the game.

2. Before beginning to play, stress the importance of really focusing on the sequence of movements, and explain how to ignore distractions.

3. Re-emphasize these concepts throughout the game.

4. Encourage the child to beat his/her average of correct sequences by utilizing ignoring, and other good attending skills.

5. Offer praise for any improvement in attending skills (especially ignoring).

24

Discussion

1. Discuss the concept and/or goal of the game. Allow the child to process feelings and thoughts he/she had while playing the game.
    * What was the most challenging aspect of this game?

2. Help the child identify things that he/she had to ignore in order to successfully play the game? (i.e. sounds in the hall, group members, telephone ringing, etc.)
    * Were these things difficult to ignore? Why?
    * How were you able to focus and ignore while playing?
    * Give one or more examples of other times one needs to focus and ignore distractions.
    * How can you remind yourself to use these skills?

Follow-Up Activity

Provide a copy of the "Watching Very Closely" worksheet (on the following page) for each student.

Watching Very Closely

Find the following words:

listen	focus	look	ask
ignore	hear	understand	think

j u y i t y e m d n s l u n d e r s t a n d k a s

s c n v d y e h d c n c v r z x a w b m l o i q

u q w x v t y m n a s p l k f b c d e e g m k k

l s w m n e r b t h i n k i u y r h z v s d f l k

i n e w f e e t h k h a l i s t e n w s x l t u y

n d b f o c u s x u e k l o o k a h t k y f g r e

v n q g y n j l o o i h e a r g d k l w b n j y r w

s f h j l m n b v c d x s d f g h y t r e w w q p

a s k n j u h b y t g v c f r r d s s a d b g r d

s r f o o g k l u s t n d i g n o r e h i n k s c m

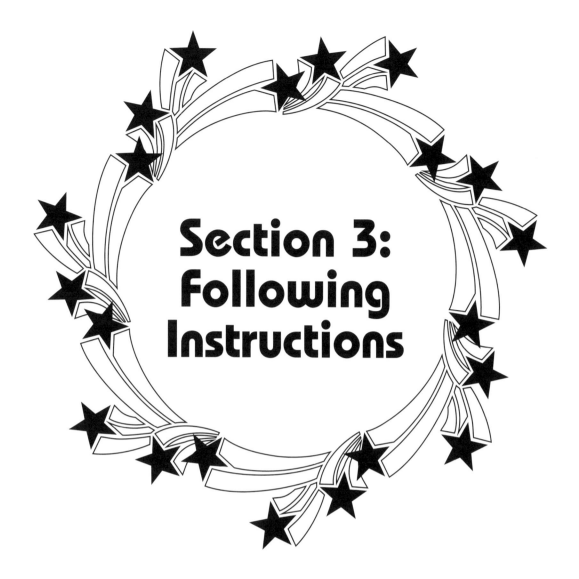

Section 3: Following Instructions

One of the chief complaints from teachers and parents alike is that children do not know how to follow instructions. Some reasons that children do not follow instructions are they do not understand or agree with the instructions, they are unable to process verbal or written instructions, and/or they do not know the instructions of a task. This section of the book provides five activities that teach children the basic skills to ensure success in the classroom and at home when following instructions.

Follow the Leader

Objective

To emphasize the importance of following directions regardless of comprehension or agreement with the directions

Grades

K-8

Game

Pick Up Sticks

Participants try to remove a stick without moving any of the other sticks in the pile. This game can be played by one or more players.

Directions

1. Play the game according to the instructions included with the game.

2. Prior to playing, tell the other player(s) that while playing the game he/she must follow your directions regarding which stick to choose.

3. Instruct the player(s) to select any stick of his/her choice a few times.

4. Give instructions of a particular color stick that the player must try to remove. (Have him/her successfully remove a few sticks before instructing him/her to attempt to remove an unlikely stick.)

5. Remind the player(s) that they must follow your directions regarding which stick is chosen.

28

Discussion

1. Discuss how it felt to be told every move to make.
    *   Did you ever disagree with the instructions that were given? Give specific examples.
    *   Why did you disagree?
    *   What did you think would have been a better choice?

2. Describe how you felt when you were given instructions to move a stick you did not think you could successfully move. Give an example of a time you had to follow directions, but you did not understand why and/or you did not agree with the directions.
    *   Did you follow the instructions anyway?
    *   What was the outcome?
    *   Were your misgivings correct, or did the situation turn out better than you had imagined it would?
    *   What did you learn from that experience?

3. Process how at times one may be instructed to do something, however one may not understand the request (for example, your mom tells you to stand very still, and do not move as she walks over and brushes some thing off your back – a spider!) and at other times, one may not agree with the instructions he/she has been given (an example would be your teacher telling everyone in the class to sit out at recess because she heard loud voices when she was outside talking with another teacher, and you were not talking), but one is still expected to follow directions.

Follow-Up Activity

Provide a copy of the "Follow the Leader" worksheet (on the following page) for each student.

[This activity is to be used with children who are slow to or refuse to follow instructions. This activity should not to be used with children who are suspected of being abused. However, it may be beneficial for you to clarify with any child that he/she should not let one do things to him/her that are not appropriate even if one is given the instruction. You may choose to have a discussion with the child about times one should not follow instructions.]

Follow the Leader

These are a few of the people whose directions I need to follow:

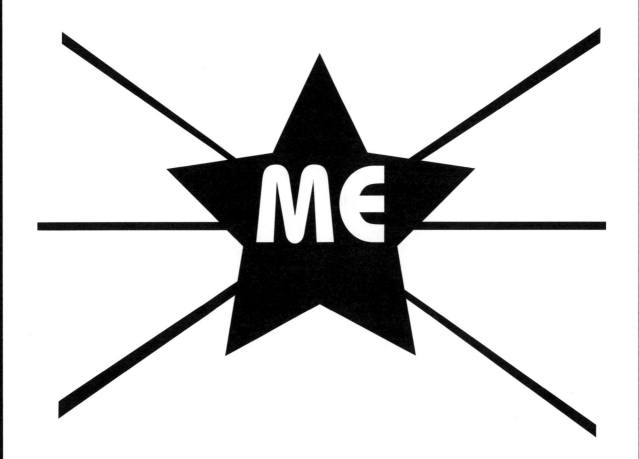

Here, There, Where?

Objective

To practice following verbal and written instructions

Grades

K-8

Game

Pick Up Sticks

Participants try to remove a stick without moving any of the other sticks in the pile. This game can be played with one or more players.

Directions

1. Give verbal instructions of things to do with the sticks. Begin with single instructions and increase as the child is successful (see page 33 for suggestions).

2. After playing a few rounds using verbal instructions, play using the written instructions provided on page 34. (Cut the strips out and allow the child to randomly choose a strip).

3. Offer encouragement when an instruction is followed.

Here, There, Where?

...Continued

Discussion

1. Was it easier for you to follow the written or the verbal instructions? Why?
   - What is involved/required for you to follow the different types of instructions? (Examples include listening, attending, following through, etc.)
   - What did you do if you forgot or did not understand an instruction? What was the result?

2. Discuss what types of instructions the child has to follow most often at home and at school.
   - What happens when you forget or make a mistake while following the instructions?
   - What could you have done to prevent receiving a consequence for not following instructions? (Example: I could have asked what the instructions were when I forgot them, instead of just guessing at what to do.)
   - Could you use the same skills used when playing this game when you need help at home or at school with instructions? (For ex. When you forgot what I said, you asked me to repeat the instructions.)
   - When can you use this at home or at school? Lead the child to give specific examples.

Follow-Up Activity

Provide a copy of the "Here, There, Where?" worksheet (on page 35) for each student.

Example Verbal Instructions
for Here, There, Where?

Single Instructions
- Make a letter "t" with two green sticks.
- Pull all of the yellow sticks out, and put them in a pile together.
- Make a square with the blue sticks.
- Make an "A" using red sticks.
- Pick up two sticks, and place them away from the other sticks.
- Pick up all the green sticks with you left hand.
- Make a shape using 6 sticks.
- Count the sticks, and tell me how many there are.
- Make your initials using the sticks.

Multiple Instructions
- Put a red stick and a blue stick in a pile together.
  Put a yellow stick and a green stick in a pile together.

- Take 2 yellow sticks and a green stick, and make a triangle using them with the point of the triangle facing down.

- Make a pile of four sticks. Take a red stick and put on top of the pile. Then, make a separate stack of the remaining yellow sticks.

- Make an "L" using a red and a blue stick. Make a "V" using green sticks, and make a "W" using yellow sticks.

- Pick up a stick with your left hand. Using your right hand, place all of the red sticks in a pile by you left foot.

- Separate the sticks into groups according to color. Take one stick from each group and make a shape. Take three more sticks from any of the groups and put them in a pile by the blue group.

- Arrange all of the sticks using a color pattern. Take the first, second, and the last sticks away from the pattern and make a triangle. Take four sticks away from the remaining pattern, and make a square to the right of the triangle.

Written Instructions
for Here, There, Where?

Make a letter "L" with two yellow sticks.	Pull all of the blue sticks out, and put them in a pile together.
Make a square with the red sticks.	Make an "A" using blue sticks.
Pick up all the yellow sticks with you left hand.	Pick up eight sticks and place them away from the other sticks.
Make a shape using 6 sticks.	Make your initials using the sticks.
Put a yellow stick and a green stick in a pile together. Put two blue sticks in a pile together.	Count the sticks and divide them into equal groups. If there are any left, put them in a pile to themselves.
Take 2 red sticks and a yellow stick and make a triangle using them with the point of the triangle facing to the left side.	Make a pile of five sticks. Take a stick and put on top of the pile. Then, make a separate stack of the remaining green sticks.
Make an "E" using a red, green, and 2 blue sticks. Make an "X" using green sticks, and make a "W" using yellow sticks.	Pick up a stick with your right hand. Using your left hand, place all of the green sticks in a pile by your right foot.
Separate the sticks into groups according to color. Take two sticks from each group and make a shape. Take 1 more stick from any of the groups and put it, along with a green stick into a pile by the blue group.	Arrange all of the sticks using a color pattern. Take the last 5 sticks away from the pattern and make a shape. Take three sticks away from the remaining pattern and make a triangle to the left of the other shape.

Here, There, Where?

Follow the Directions:

- Draw a circle in the middle of the shape below, and color it blue.

- Make a triangle in the bottom right hand corner, and color it orange.

- Color the background of the entire space yellow.

- Write your name at the top of this page in the upper left hand corner.

- Write the following sentence at the bottom of the page, "I am great at following instructions!"

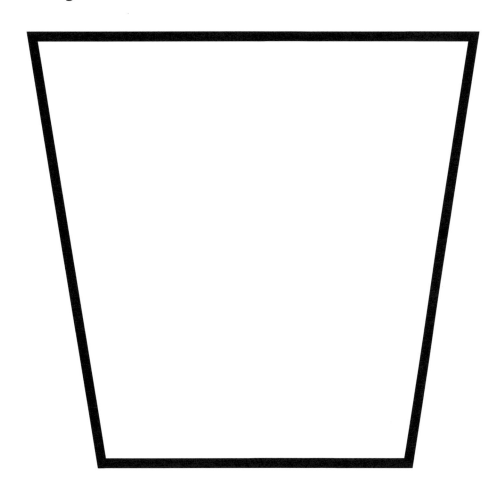

Listening & Being Still at the Same Time

Objective

To introduce the concept of following two directives at one time

Grades

2-8

Game

Connect Four®

Participants try to connect four chips vertically, horizontally, or diagonally. This game can be played with two people at a time.

Directions

1. Play according to the instructions included with the game.

2. Pause at times to discuss the child's strategy of play.

3. Play one time with the child trying only to get four chips in a row.

4. Play again with the child trying only to block you from getting four in a row.

5. Play the game with the child incorporating both objectives.

6. Offer praise when the child demonstrates dual thinking not winning.

36

Discussion

1. Once it becomes apparent that one person is about to win, pause play and discuss the strategy being used. Oftentimes, one player takes a defensive stance and the other an offensive stance. Discuss the differences between playing offensively and defensively.

2. Have the child identify if they are playing just to get four in a row or if they are playing just to block your moves.
   • What are the advantages and/or disadvantages to his/her strategy?

3. Explore any feelings the child has about having to play to get four chips in a row while preventing you from doing the same. For example, "How do you feel when you realize that not only do you have to get four in a row, but you also have to keep me from getting four in a row?"

4. Have the child identify real-life situations that require thinking about at least two things at one time. (Examples: read silently without talking; listen and be still; listen and write notes at the same time)

Follow-Up Activity

Provide a copy of the "Listening and Being Still At the Same Time" worksheet (on the following page) for each student.

Listening & Being Still at the Same Time

Draw a picture of yourself doing one thing.

Draw a picture of yourself doing
two things at one time.

Say That Again

Objective

To practice following instructions that are given verbally

Grades

K-8

Game

Twister®

Participants are given instructions to follow that involve putting their hands/feet on certain colored circles. This game can be played with two or more people.

Directions

1. Play a few rounds following the instructions included with the game.

2. Next, play the game by giving a sequence of verbal instructions. (Instruction suggestions are provided on page 41). Continue increasing the number of instructions given at one time based on the skills of the child. Also, occasionally give an instruction using a low tone of voice or by stating it very fast.

3. When giving multiple instructions, let the child take notes prior to following through with the instructions.

4. Offer feedback and encouragement when instructions are followed.

Say That Again

...Continued

Discussion

1. What was easy and/or hard when playing with only one direction given at a time?
   • What did you do if you did not hear or understand an instruction?

2. What was different when playing with multiple instructions given at one time?
   • What did you do to try to remember the instructions?
   • When you were allowed to take notes did that help any?

3. Describe a situation in which you are given verbal instructions (when taking a test, parents asking you to do something, etc.).
   • Do you always follow through with their instructions or do you forget sometimes?
   • When you are having trouble following through with instructions that are given verbally, what are some things that you can do to help you?

Follow-Up Activity

Provide a copy of the "Say That Again" worksheet (on the following page) for each student.

Sequence Instruction Suggestions for Say That Again

Put your left foot on blue and your left hand on red

Put your left hand on blue, your right hand on green

Put your left foot on red, your right hand on blue, and your right foot on yellow

Put your right hand on yellow and sit on green

Place your left foot on green, your right foot on green, your left hand on red, and your right hand on red

Put your right thumb on blue, your left pinky on red, and both feet on yellow

Sit on red, put your right foot on blue, your left foot on yellow. Now, stand and put both feet on green

Put your right foot on blue, your left foot on yellow, your right hand on red, your left hand on green

Sit on yellow, put your right hand on green, your left hand on red, and your left foot on blue

Put your right knee on green, your left hand on blue, and your right hand on red

Stand with both feet on yellow, one hand on blue, and one hand one red. Stand up, turn around and stand on green

Put your left hand on yellow, your right hand on blue, your left foot on green, your right foot on yellow, and then stand and face the door

Say That Again

1. Cut out the bottom half of the sheet and give to the child.
2. Instruct the child to follow the instructions that you give:
    - Color the eyes blue
    - Color the lips orange
    - Color the nose yellow.
    - Color the dot closest to the top green.
    - Color the dot closest to the head blue.
    - Color the dot at the far right brown.
    - Name the bug. Write the name under its legs.
    - Decorate the bottom dots with black polka dots.

- -

What Do I Do?

Objective

To establish the importance of knowing the instructions prior to beginning and/or completing tasks

Grades

K-8

Game

Simon®

Participants try to successfully repeat a pattern modeled by the game. This game can be played with one or more people.

Directions

1. Play the game according to the instructions included with the game.

2. After playing a few rounds according to the instructions, blindfold the child, and allow him/her to play a few rounds.

3. Offer feedback and encouragement during the session.

Discussion

1. When playing the first few rounds, how did you know which button to push next in the sequence?

What Do I Do?

...Continued

- What was hard about playing the game this way?
  Did you feel like you had some success?
- What was different when you played blindfolded?
- Was there any way that you could have gotten the sequences right by not following the pattern of the game? (Could you have just hit buttons at random and got the right answer?)

2. Discuss how playing this game is similar to situations in life. For example, in order to follow instructions at home or at school, one first has to know what the instructions are. This is just like playing the game—in order to get the sequences correct, one has to know which button is included in the sequence.

- What are the advantages to knowing what the instructions are before you start something?
- Tell about a time that you did something without following the directions exactly right. What happened as a result?
- Relate how doing things without knowing the instructions is just like trying to play this game blindfolded.
- What could you do if you read or heard instructions and you still did not know what to do?

Follow-Up Activity

Provide a copy of the "What Do I Do?" worksheet (on the following page) for each student.

What Do I Do?

Read each question. Circle true or false.

1. I should read the instructions
    only if I need help or don't
    understand something.

    True or False?

2. I should ask someone for help if I
   don't understand the instructions.

   True or False?

3. It is always okay to make
    up my own instructions when
    doing a task.

    True or False?

Section 4:
Impulsivity

At one time or another we have all struggled with impulsivity. Impulsive behaviors include speaking without waiting one's turn, acting on an impulse (urge) without thinking, rushing ahead without waiting for instructions, and so on. In order to be able to effectively cope with the sudden urge an impulse brings, children need to be taught specific skills that help them process events and act accordingly. This section of the book provides seven activities that are designed to teach children successful ways of managing impulses. The activities specifically focus on bringing to awareness situations in which one feels impulsive, teaching one to learn to take his or her time by processing the consequences of rushing through tasks, and establishing the importance of thinking prior to acting.

On Your Mark, Get Set, Done!

Objective

To develop skills to remind oneself to take his or her time when completing a task

Grades

K-8

Game

Perfection®

Participants try to place 25 shapes on the board within sixty seconds or less. This game can be played with two – eight people.

Directions

1. Play the game according to the instructions included with the game.

2. After each round of playing the game, process how he or she feels and what he or she was thinking.

3. Introduce the following skill steps:
    a. Recognize when you feel the need to rush.
    b. Take a deep breath.
    c. Give yourself a reason why you should take your time.
    d. Continue with the task.

Discussion

1. During processing after a round, ask how it feels to know that you are being timed?
   - What are you thinking, feeling, etc.?
   - How would playing the game be different if you were not timed? Provide an opportunity for the child to play the game with no time constraints. Continue to process what is different.

2. How do you know when you want to rush through a task or when you feel rushed?
   - How do you feel inside?
   - What are you thinking?
   - How does your body feel?
   - Following identification of the above, tie in the first step of how he or she is able to identify the need to rush. Brainstorm ideas of certain things that could act as cues to remind himself/herself she may want to slow down.

3. Once you recognize that you feel the need to rush, what are things you could do next? Teach the concept of deep breathing and practice.
   - Play rounds of the game in which you prompt the child to take deep breaths. Process how it felt after taking deep breaths. Practice reciting the first two skill steps.

4. What are some reasons you should take your time? After brainstorming several general reasons, provide more specific tasks that the child is

presently engaged in. For example, ask, "Why is it important for you not to rush when completing your math test in Ms. X's room?" Review the third skill step. Provide practice opportunities by reciting a task and asking the child to give a rationale. Practice reciting the three skill steps.

5. How is a task or activity completed? Discuss the concept of completion as being a step-by-step (problem by problem) process, just as in the game of Perfection®, you put one piece in at a time. Ask the child to put all the pieces into the game at once (not piece by piece). Process what happens (it is a mess and usually none are in the appropriate places). Follow up by asking the child to place the shapes in one at a time. What is different? Reinforce the last skill step of continuing with the task.

6. Practice stating all four skill steps. Discuss how one can use these steps in real situations.
    • What will be hard and/or easy about using these steps?
      Provide opportunities to role-play using the skill steps.

Follow-Up Activity

Provide a copy of the "On Your Mark, Get Set, Done!" worksheet (on the following page) for each student.

On Your Mark, Get Set, Done!

The 4 Skill Steps:

1. _____
2. _____
3. _____
4. _____

This is a situation in which I need to use the 4 skill steps

_____.

This is a picture of me taking my time to finish:

Rush Hour

Objective

To identify times and/or situations in which one wants to rush through things

Grades

K-8

Game

Ants in the Pants®

Participants try to make their ants jump into the pants. This game can be played with two – eight people.

Directions

1. Give each player an equal number of ants.
2. Allow the participants to try to make their ants jump in the pants while engaged in discussion.
3. Offer positive feedback as often as possible.
4. If one is unable to talk and play the game at the same time, have him or her try to make the ants jump after offering an answer or comment.

Discussion

1. What does it mean when someone says you act like you have ants in your pants? Describe times when you feel like you have ants in your pants.

Rush Hour

...Continued

2. Engage in a discussion about how sometimes we feel like we have ants in our pants when we are excited or when we feel bored. Describe a time when you were so excited about something that you did not want to take your time doing anything else. (For example, one may have rushed through an assignment in order to be able to watch a movie in class).
    -   What happened as a result of you rushing through the task?
    -   What do you usually do when you get bored with a particular task?

3. Reinforce that feeling excited and/or bored (or having "ants in your pants") is not 'bad'. One just needs to recognize that when these situations occur he or she should be aware that special steps may need to be made in order to get the outcome he or she desires.

Follow-Up Activity

Provide a copy of the "Rush Hour" worksheet (on the following page) for each student.

Rush Hour

On each ant's tail, write times when you feel the need to rush. On the large ant on the bottom, write a reminder for yourself to take time to enjoy things and do your best, without rushing! Cut out the large ant, and put it some-where that it will serve as a reminder of today's lesson.

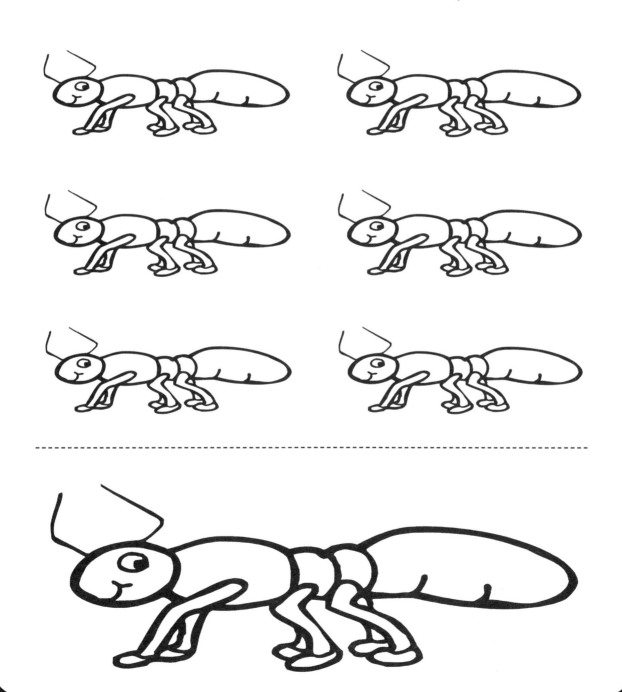

Slow & Steady Wins the Race

Objective

To establish the importance of one learning to take his or her time when completing a task

Grades

K-8

Game

Operation®

Participants use tweezers to remove parts from the game board without touching the sides. This game can be played with two – eight people.

Directions

1. Play the game according to the instructions provided with the game.

2. Point out specific behaviors exhibited during the session that is evidence one is taking his or her time when playing the game and/or during discussion time.

3. Provide encouragement throughout the session.

4. An alternate way to play is to set a timer and see how many parts can be successfully removed in different time increments.

Discussion

1. What skills are important to remember when you play this game? Describe how each of those is important to playing the game. For example, one may say it is important to hold the tweezers with one hand. This is important because it is much easier to touch the sides when holding the tweezers with both hands.
   - Are you more likely to make mistakes when you rush playing this game or when you take your time? Why?

2. When the timer is used, process after each timed segment how he or she felt.
   - Did you feel rushed during the shorter timed segments?

3. What are some jobs, activities, or assignments that you have to complete that require you to take your time?
   - How do you feel when you take your time on an activity versus when you do not take your time?
   - Why is it important that you take your time on each job, activity, or assignment?

4. What are some careers/jobs that require one to take his or her time? Follow up with each job listed and pursue why it is important? For example, if a doctor is listed, ask what might happen if he rushes through a visit so that he can go home sooner?
   - When do you think these people learned to take their time?
   - Brainstorm advantages why one should learn to take his or her time when he or she is young.

Follow-Up Activity

Provide a copy of the "Slow & Steady Wins the Race" worksheet (on the following page) for each student.

Slow & Steady

Color the pictures that apply to you.

These are situations that I rush through at home:

Chores

Homework

Personal Care

Other:_____

Time with
My Family

These are situations that I rush through at school:

Classwork

Tests

Study Time

Activity Time

Other:_____

This week, I will slow down, and take my time when I
_____.

Strengthen the Tower

Objective

To demonstrate that taking one's time when completing a task generally produces more positive results than rushing through a task

Grades

K-8

Game

Jenga®

Participants work together to build the tower as high as possible. This game can be played with two – eight people.

Directions

1. Have each person stack blocks vertically to see how high he/she is able to build a tower.

2. Look for opportunities to encourage and offer feedback.

3. After trying to build the blocks vertically a few times, brainstorm ways one could make the tower stronger, and implement the ideas.

4. Do comparisons by instructing for a tower to be built in 10 seconds versus a tower being built in 40 seconds, etc.

Strengthen the Tower
...Continued

Discussion

1. Have a discussion about how we sometimes want to rush through things.
   - What are the positive and negative consequences of rushing through a task?
   - Describe a time you rushed through a task.
   - Would you have been more successful if you would have taken your time? How?

2. After playing according to direction #3, emphasize the time spent planning and constructing the new ideas.
   - What would happen if we used one of the new ideas, but we rushed to try to build it? (use in coordination with direction #4)

3. Identify one activity at home or at school in which taking your time will help you be more successful.
   - How can you remind yourself to take your time during the selected activity?
   - What will be the benefits of taking your time?

Follow-Up Activity

Provide a copy of the "Strengthen the Tower" worksheet (on the following page) for each student.

Strengthen
the Tower

In the blocks below, write advantages
of taking your time when doing tasks.

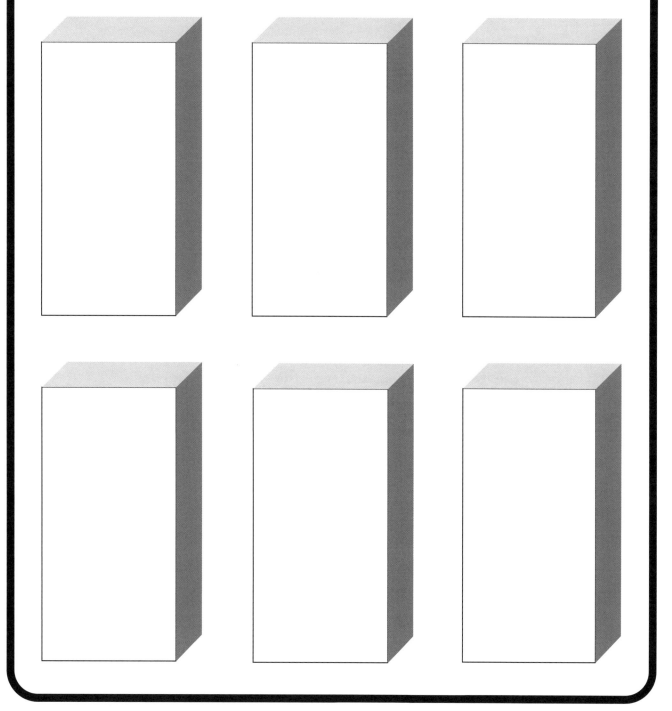

Think Before You Speak

Objective

To aid in the development of the skill to think before speaking

Grades

3-8

Game

Taboo®

Teams provide verbal cues for the given word in a limited amount of time. Also, there are certain words that cannot be used when giving clues. This game can be played with two – four pairs of people.

Directions

1. Play according to the instructions included with the game.

2. Before playing, give an example of a topic with a shorter time limit to demonstrate the importance of giving clues as quickly as possible.

3. Allow play to begin and go on for three rounds.

4. Process how difficult/challenging it is to think of clues in a given amount of time.

5. Suggest that the child use the few seconds before the time starts to brainstorm possible clues.

6. Restart the game, allowing 5-10 seconds of time for the child to brainstorm.

7. Play for a determined length of time.

Discussion

1. Did brainstorming clues before playing make it easier? How?

2. How did you feel when your partner could not guess the correct answer?

3. When brainstorming, did you consider if your partner would be able to understand and/or relate to your clues?
   • Were you surprised at how your clues were interpreted by your partner? Describe.

4. Describe some everyday situations in which you need to brainstorm before speaking.
   • Tell of a time when you spoke before thinking? What was the result?
   • What are some things that you can do to help catch yourself when you are tempted to speak before thinking?

Follow-Up Activity

Provide a copy of the "Think Before You Speak" worksheet (on the following page) for each student.

Think Before You Speak

Describe a situation where what you said and what you meant to say were two different things.

I said _____.

I meant to say_____.

List as many ways as possible that you can remind yourself to think before you speak.

This week, I will try to_____ before I speak.

Think, Think, Think

Objective

To increase one's ability to evaluate situations before acting

Grades

K-8

Game

Jenga®

Participants work together to build the tower as high as possible. This game can be played with two – eight people.

Directions

1. Play according to the instructions included with the game.

2. Demonstrate how to choose a block from the tower.

3. While playing the game, engage in conversation that relates the game to the objective.

4. Throughout the game, give encouragement when a careful selection is made, even if the tower falls, in an effort to reinforce the thinking component.

Discussion

1. What would happen if you pulled out a block that was not loose?
   - Emphasize that pulling out a block that is not loose could make the tower unstable, or it may fall. Sometimes when we act too quickly, things happen that we did not expect or want to happen.

2. How can you determine if a block is loose or not? One can look at the block, touch it, or look at the surrounding blocks.
   - Discuss how one can determine if a behavior is appropriate in a given situation.

3. Tell about a situation at home or at school in which you knew that if you did or did not do something, you would get into trouble. Further discuss how they knew prior to the action/inaction they would receive a consequence. Point out certain blocks in the tower and discuss what would specifically happen if that block was pulled. For effect, follow through by asking the child to pull one of the blocks out after the discussion.
   - What are some things that you can do to remind yourself to think about a situation before you act?

Follow-Up Activity

Provide a copy of the "Think, Think, Think" worksheet (on the following page) for each student.

Think, Think, Think

Copy the bookmark outline onto colored paper or construction paper.

Allow the child to write reminders for himself/herself to think about situations before acting.

Allow time for him/her to decorate the bookmark.

Objective

To establish the importance of waiting for instructions and clarifications before rushing ahead

Grades

3-8

Game

Hangman®

Participants try to guess an opponents word. With each try that passes without a correct answer, the "man" gets a step nearer to being hanged. This game can be played with two – eight people.

Directions

1. Discuss the objective and the rules of the game with the child.

2. Play a round following the instructions included with the game.

3. Explain that the next round will be played following different directions. Tell the child that neither of you will guess letters. Each time, you will try to guess the entire word.

Discussion

1. After playing the round following the instructions, discuss what is easy and/or difficult about playing the game.
   - Did you find yourself trying to guess the word after you got one letter? What was the result?
   - How were you finally able to guess the word? Emphasize the concept of how in order to guess the word you have to pay attention to the situation instead of just randomly guessing. For example, one has to consider how many letters are in the word and what letters are/are not in the word.
   - What would happen if you just started guessing words, but did not even pay attention to how many letters were actually in the word?

2. After playing the second round with the new directions, discuss what was more difficult playing this way.
   - Were you able to guess the word without having any letters? Describe a situation in which you sometimes want to jump ahead and do things without having all the information or without having to wait. (Examples may include: Being the first to line up for lunch, starting assignments without having all the instructions, etc.)
   - What happens when you go ahead and do these things without waiting for the instructions or having all the necessary information?
   - What would have happened if I put this game in front of you and just said, "play?" Would you have known exactly what to do and where to put all the letters, etc.?
   - When you find yourself in a situation in which you are tempted to rush ahead, what should you do?
   - How can you remind yourself of what you should do in those situations?

Follow-Up Activity

Provide a copy of the "Waiting Around" worksheet (on the following page) for each student.

Waiting Around

Read all of the directions FIRST!

List problems that could happen if you do not wait for instructions:

Name at least 2 examples of times you
did not wait for instructions:

1. _____

2. _____

Give at least 3 ways you can remind yourself
to wait for instructions:

1. _____

2. _____

3. _____

Turn the page over and write all of your
answers 3 more times.

Write your name at the top of the page, and do not
answer any of the questions. Pat yourself on the back,
because you read the directions first!

Section 5:
Making
Decisions

On a daily basis, individuals are faced with making many decisions. Some decisions can be made with only a little effort while other decisions require careful thought and consideration. This section seeks to equip children with the skills critical to making good decisions. The five activities focus on teaching children how to ask for help, how to evaluate the consequences certain of decisions, and how to gather all the facts about a situation before making a decision.

Help, Please.

Objective

To encourage one to ask for help when needed in making decisions

Grades

K-8

Game

Bop It®/Bop It Extreme®

Participants quickly try to follow oral instructions given by the game. This game can be played with two – eight people.

Directions

1. Play according to the instructions included with the game.

2. After playing a few rounds, encourage students to discuss how they played the game.

3. Offer frequent encouragement as the child makes an effort to play the game (which is often frustrating).

Discussion

1. How did you know what to do each time during the game?
   - What would have happened if you just "guessed" at what to do each time?

2. When you make decisions, how do you usually go about making a choice? Tell about a time you had to make a hard decision and you did not know what to do. Did you get help from anyone? If so, how did you go about seeking their help, and what did you do afterwards?

3. Discuss the importance of getting outside help when making decisions instead of just randomly choosing (just as the voice in the game helps you make decisions, so can another person that you trust).
   - What are some decisions that would require you to ask for help from someone?
   - How would you be able to determine who to ask for help in a given situation?
   - What characteristics would they need to have? Role-play ways one could ask for help using different situations or using problems relevant to the child's situation.

Follow-Up Activity

Provide a copy of the "Help, Please." worksheet (on the following page) for each student.

Help, Please.

List people that you could trust to ask for
help with making a decision.

At school: _____   _____

_____   _____

At home: _____   _____

_____   _____

Draw a picture of yourself asking someone for help.

Oh, No!

Objective

To demonstrate how decisions sometimes produce unintended consequences

Grades

K-8

Game

Don't Break the Ice®

Participants take turns knocking blocks of ice out of the game board while trying not to make the skater fall. This game can be played with two – eight people.

Directions

1. Play the game according to the instructions included with the game.

2. Offer feedback and encouragement during the session.

Oh, No!

...Continued

Discussion

1. When one hits a block of ice that makes more than one block fall, discuss how that happened? Was it intended?
    *   What did you think would happen? What might have prevented the other blocks from falling? Relate the situation to how we sometimes make choices that have unintended consequences. Discuss how our choices can affect our future, as well as other people. Share a personal example about unintended consequences, and ask the child to share. In the situations shared, what might have prevented the unintended consequence(s)?

2. What should one do after he or she has made a decision that resulted in unintended consequences that affected one's: family, friends, and/or future? Sometimes, it will be more beneficial to provide scenarios for the child to determine the appropriate course of action instead of asking generically.

Follow-Up Activity

Provide a copy of the "Oh, No!" worksheet (on the following page) for each student. For younger students, read the scenarios for them and allow them to verbally give the answers.

Oh, No!

Read the following scenarios, and write what you would do in each situation.

1. You wanted a book that was on the top shelf in your room. Instead of asking for help, you stood on the lower shelf to reach for the book. When you did, the shelf, along with everything on it, fell over. Your mom hears the noise and comes running to your room.

_____

_____

_____

2. You made a new friend at school today. You spent lots of time trying to get to know him/her. However, your best friend got mad at you because it appeared that you were ignoring him/her.

_____

_____

_____

3. You have been saving your money to buy something that cost $20. You had saved $5. You went to the store, and without thinking, you spent $4.35.

_____

_____

_____

Private Eye

Objective

To discuss the importance of learning the details of a situation before making a decision.

Grades

2-8

Game

Guess Who®

Participants try to guess the character of the other person by asking investigative questions about the character. This game can be played with two – eight people. If played with more than two, teams should be used.

Directions

1. Play the game according to the instructions included with the game.

2. An alternate way to play is to draw a card, and let the child verbally describe the person as you try to guess the person, and vice versa.

3. Offer continual encouragement and feedback as the game is played.

Discussion

1. How did you decide what questions to ask me about my character?
   - What would have happened if you just decided to put some of the characters down without asking me a question regarding them?

2. After playing the game using the alternate directions (see direction #2), discuss how one would know whom to guess. Based on the description, were you able to rule out certain people? How? Tell about a decision that you have to make daily or will have to make in the future.
   - How do you or will you go about making the decision? Discuss the importance of learning about the situation (knowing the details) before making a discussion.
   - Relate the gathering of information to a court hearing. Why do you think the court uses so much time to listen to evidence in a case before making a decision? What might happen if they did not take the time to hear evidence or learn about the case?

3. If you are unsure about a situation or the details regarding the circumstance, what can you do? How can you go about learning?

Follow-Up Activity

Provide a copy of the "Private Eye" worksheet (on the following page) for each student.

Private Eye

Find the following items in the picture below.

The Good, the Bad & the Ugly

Objective

To develop the ability to weigh possible outcomes when making a decision

Grades

2-8

Game

Battleship®

Participants try to sink an opponent's ships by calling out coordinates. This game can be played with two – four people per game.

Directions

1. Play according to the instructions included with the game.

2. Discuss various points to consider before naming coordinates (do they have an idea based on a previous selection where a hit could occur?)

3. Engage the child in conversation about success or lack of.

4. During the game, continue to point out clues the child may not notice about where their opponent may have a ship. For example, if a child gets a hit on B1 & B2, he or she has a good chance of scoring another hit on B3 as opposed to choosing a random coordinate.

Discussion

1. Did you randomly choose coordinates, or did you have a pattern? (ex.: first of each letter, etc.?) Explore the child's rationale for choosing his or her coordinates. Explain the rationale you used in making choices. Continue the discussion by asking if his or her rationale was successful or not and why? Discuss any clues the child may have missed (ex. you had a hit on B1, B2, but you never called B3 and that would have sunk my destroyer).

2. Help the child relate the game to an experience at home or school where they had to look for "clues" and determine if they should continue with their original choice or make changes. Discuss how in some situations, there may not be an obvious "good" choice. As in the game before a hit, any choice of coordinates may seem "bad."

Follow-Up Activity

Provide a copy of the "The Good, the Bad, & the Ugly" worksheet (on the following page) for each student.

The Good, the Bad, and the Ugly

Read the following scenario. Write all the possible positive outcomes on the arrow pointing up, and write all the possible negative outcomes on the arrow pointing down.

You borrowed a video game from your friend. You did not tell your mom because she does not allow you to do that. On your way back to return the game, you accidentally fell, and the game broke.

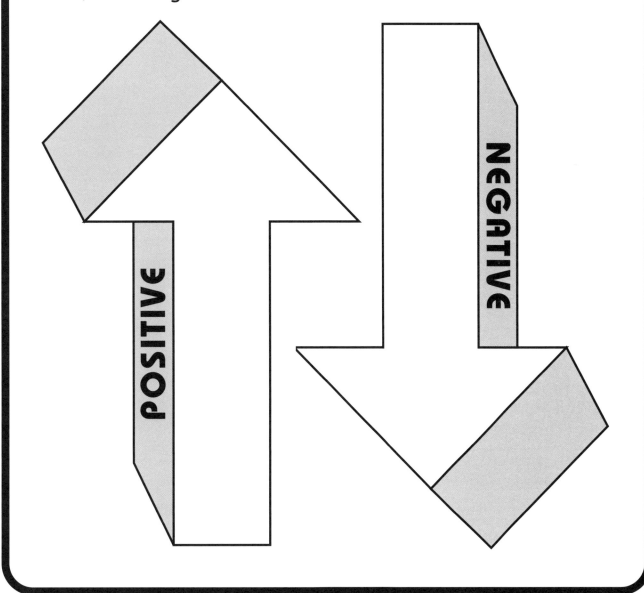

POSITIVE

NEGATIVE

Weighing Choices

Objective

To teach the concept of considering the pros and cons of choices when making decisions

Grades

K-8

Game

Don't Spill the Beans®

Participants try to stack as many beans as possible onto the bowl without making it tip over. This game can be played with two – four people per game.

Directions

1. Play the game according to the instructions included with the game.

2. Continually relate the concept of the game back to the objective.

3. Once you have introduced the concept of pros and cons, you may want to play the game differently. Take all the beans from the game. Place a slip of paper in one tray that says pros and a slip of paper in the other tray that says cons. When a pro is named for a given problem, place a bean in the pro tray. When a con is listed, place a bean in the con tray. Point out how one wants to make the choice that has the most beans in the pro tray.

4. Offer feedback and encouragement throughout the session.

Discussion

1. What is the objective of the game? (to keep the bowl from tipping over)
   - Is there anything you can do to help keep the bowl from tipping over?
   - Is there anything that you can do to make the bowl tip over?
   - After discussing the above two questions, emphasize that one choice produces positive results whereas the other choice produces negative results.

2. What are some choices you have to make on a daily basis? Have the child tell about his/her easiest and hardest decisions that he/she has ever made. Discuss what makes some decisions hard and some easy.

3. When you have a decision to make, how do you go about making a choice? Discuss how with each decision there are usually good choices, better choices, and "not-so-good" choices.
   - How do you determine if a choice is good, better, or not-so-good? Introduce the concept of pros & cons. (What positive things will happen if I choose…What negative things will happen if I choose…)

4. Play according to direction #3. Ask the child to identify a choice he/she has to make (or have him/her make up a choice). Then, follow the direction, allowing the child to "see" which one may be a better choice.

Follow-Up Activity

Provide a copy of the "Weighing Choices" worksheet (on the following page) for each student.

Weighing Choices

In the space below, describe a decision you are going to have to make in the near future. Decide what choice you think you will make. In the cans below, write the pros and cons of the choice.

The Decision

_____

_____

_____

The Choice

_____

_____

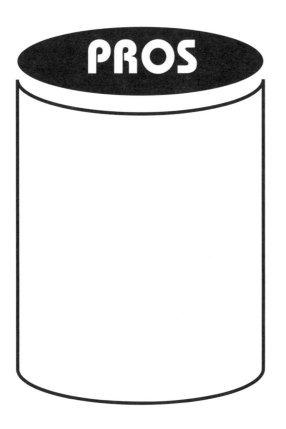

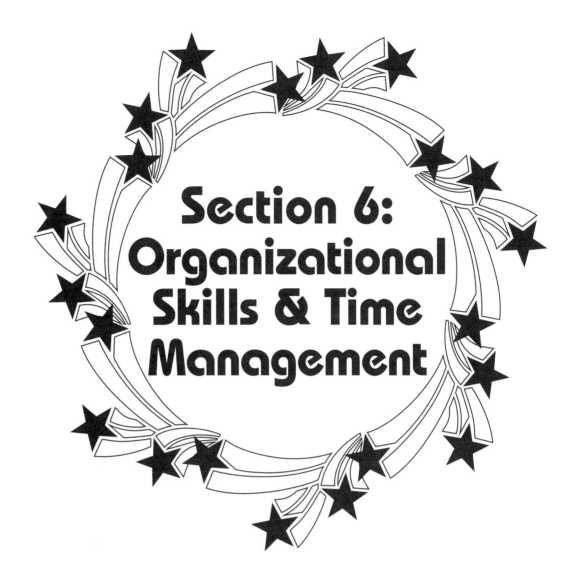

Section 6: Organizational Skills & Time Management

Multi-tasking is a popular phrase, but it is only intended for adults, right? No! Children are busier than ever. With school and extracurricular activities, they need help with time-management, too. Schools, daycares, and families are also facing increasing numbers of children diagnosed with ADHD (Attention Deficit-Hyperactive Disorder) of which poor organizational skills are a determining criterion. However, organizational skills/time management is often a neglected lesson for children. The games and activities in this section assist children with organizing materials before starting a task, writing reminder notes to themselves, and completing a task in a pre-determined amount of time.

A,B,C 1,2,3

Objective

To emphasize the importance of organizing one's self and materials prior to beginning a task

Grades

K-8

Game

Go Fish Card Game

Players ask each other for cards to make a matched set, and the first person to match all his/her cards is the winner. This can be played with two - eight people per deck of cards.

Directions

1. Play using a standard deck of playing cards, and using the traditional rules for Go Fish. (Each player is dealt 5 cards. Everyone then takes turns asking another player for a number he/she needs to make a matching pair; if the other player does not have the requested card, he/she says "go fish," and the player draws one card from the deck. It is then another players turn. This continues until one player matches all his/her cards.)

2. Instruct the players to begin playing. (Do not allow them to organize their cards – tell them to stop if they try.)

3. Play a second time, but first have all players organize/group their cards by number or suit.

Discussion Topics

1. Was it more difficult to determine which cards you needed, or if you had a requested card during the first round of play (prior to organizing)? Was it easier to locate a card after organizing your cards?

2. Do you have any areas in your life (home or school) where you are organized? Describe.
   - What are the benefits of being organized?
   - What are some of the disadvantages of being disorganized?

3. Do you have any areas in your life where you are not organized? Describe.
   - Brainstorm ways to become more organized in one area this week.

Follow Up

Provide a copy of the "A,B,C,1,2,3" worksheet (on the following page) for each student.

A,B,C, 1,2,3

Pretend that you are in charge of organizing all the things on this page. Group the items into the categories listed below by coloring each item the appropriate color.

1. Things that would go in a house (Red)
2. Shapes that are rounded (Yellow)
3. Arrows (Blue)
4. Shapes that are square (Green)

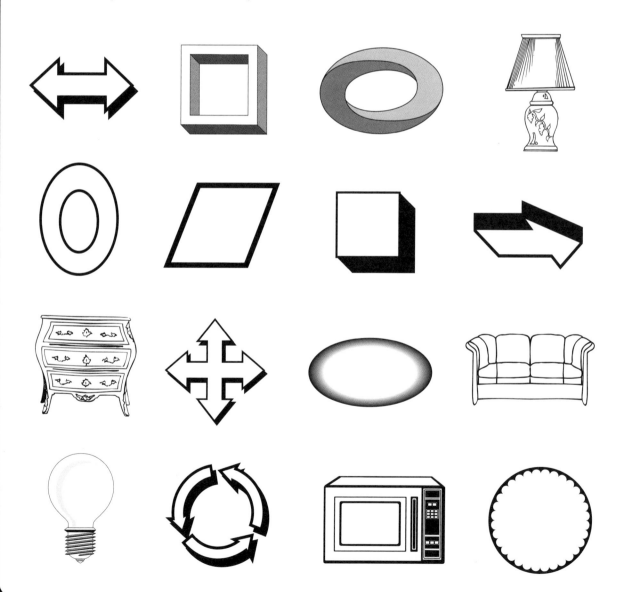

Get Your Ducks In A Row

Objective

To assist in organizing materials prior to an activity so that one's time is used wisely

Grades

K-8

Game

Guesstures®

Participants act-out words in a limited amount of time. This game can be played with two – eight people.

Directions

1. Play the game according to the instructions included with the game.

2. Before beginning to play, emphasize the importance of the order of the words, by asking the children to brainstorm possible clues they will give to assist them in identifying which words are easiest or more difficult for them.

3. If after 1 or 2 rounds it becomes obvious that the child is not going to be successful, play without placing the cards in the Mimer Timer, to take away the time constraints.
   a. Once the child is successful without the timer, gradually introduce a time limit (this can be done with a clock at first, and with longer time frames).

b. Continue to gradually decrease the time limit until the child can play with the Mimer Timer and have some success.
— This process may take more than one session

4. Encourage a few minutes of organizing his/her thoughts before beginning each turn.

5. Challenge the child to beat his/her record on each turn.

6. Praise his/her organizational skills.

Discussion

1. Do you feel that organizing your thoughts and/or words helped you?

2. How did you organize your thoughts and/or words?

3. Identify and discuss activities that require organization (cleaning a room, getting ready for school on time, taking a test, etc.).

4. Identify at least 1 activity in which you could possibly be more successful if you were more organized before beginning.
   • How will you organize yourself before this activity?

Follow-Up Activity

Provide a copy of the "Get Your Ducks In a Row" worksheet (on the following page) for each student.

Get Your Ducks in a Row

_____ is an activity that I need to be more organized before beginning.

These are the steps I can take to become more organized:

When I am more organized, I am more likely to finish the job. This week, I will become more organized with

_____.

Just a Reminder

Objective

To demonstrate how to remind oneself to do certain things

Grades

2-8

Game

Memory®

Participants try to find matching pairs of cards. This game can be played with two – eight people.

Directions

1. Play according to the instructions included with the game.

2. After turns have passed in which participants were unable to match cards that had previously been turned over, allow the child to write himself/herself a reminder as to where the cards are. (This is easier if the cards are initially laid out in columns and rows. Examples may be: sun – 3rd row, 1st card; train – last card, 7th row)

3. Offer encouragement throughout the session.

Discussion

1. When playing without writing reminders was it harder? Why?
   - How did the reminders help you? Do you think writing the reminders helped enough for you to justify the time you spent writing them?

2. What are some things that you often forget to do?
   - What happens when you forget to do those things?
   - What are some ways you could help remind yourself to do them? Discuss how in the game, one wrote reminders. Talk about different ways one could write reminders about the things he/she discussed. (Examples are provided on pages 95, 96.)
   - Where are places you should put the reminders or how can you remember to use the reminders?

Follow-Up Activity

Provide a copy of the "Just a Reminder" worksheet (on the following page) for each student.

Just a Reminder

I need to learn to remember to

_____.

This week, I can help remind myself to do this by

_____.

In the box below or on another sheet,
create yourself a reminder.

- -

Just a Reminder

An example of a reminder one could use:

To Do List

At Home: _____
_____
_____
_____
_____

At School: _____
_____
_____
_____
_____

Other: _____
_____
_____
_____

Just a Reminder

An example of a reminder one could use:

To Do List

Sunday _____
_____
_____

Monday _____
_____
_____

Tuesday _____
_____
_____

Wednesday _____
_____
_____

Thursday _____
_____
_____

Friday _____
_____
_____

Saturday _____
_____
_____

Time Is Up!

Objective

To assist one in developing skills necessary to complete an activity within a predetermined time

Grades

K-8

Game

Perfection®

Participants try to place 25 shapes on the board within sixty seconds or less. This game can be played with one – eight people.

Directions

1. Play the game according to the instructions included with the game.

2. If the child is able to get all of the pieces on the board within the first few rounds, challenge the child to continue to beat his/her time.

3. If the child has difficulty getting all the pieces on the board in the given time, take his/her average number of pieces left and have the child get one more each time until all the pieces are in. This method can be used with or without the timer.

Time Is Up!

...Continued

4. Another alternate method for a child who is having a difficult time is to remove only 1/4 or 1/2 of the game pieces and continue to add 1-2 more pieces when he/she proves successful until the child can place all the pieces. Again, this method can be used with or without the timer.

Discussion

1. Which pieces were the hardest for you to place?

2. How did you feel when playing this game?

3. Ask the child to relate this experience to a situation in the classroom or at home. Process the strategy/steps he/she used to be more successful (add comments from your observations during the game). Suggest possible strategies, such as: grouping pieces by shape, picking up 2 or more pieces at a time, leaving the most difficult for last, etc.).

5. How can he/she use this same strategy in the classroom or at home?

Follow-Up Activity

Provide a copy of the "Time Is Up" worksheet (on the following page) for each student.

Just a Reminder

I have trouble completing _____ on time.

List in the clocks things that you can do to help you finish on time.

When I finish something on time, I feel _____!

What Do I Need?

Objective

To demonstrate how when one has the needed materials before starting a task, tasks can be accomplished in less time

Grades

K-8

Game

Barrel of Monkeys®

Participants try to form a chain using the monkeys. This game can be played with two – eight people.

Directions

1. Play the game according to the instructions included with the game. When the child is ready to play the game for the first time, spread the monkeys out in different places around the room. Time the round, and record it on a piece of paper.

2. Next, allow the child to play the game with the monkeys placed in color sets in different places throughout the room. Record the time it takes to complete the round onto the piece of paper.

3. Allow the child to play with all the monkeys placed in a pile near him/her. Record the time it takes to complete the round onto the piece of paper.

4. Offer encouragement throughout the game process and through the remainder of the session.

100

Discussion

1. What was difficult about playing the game during the first round?
   - What did you spend most of your time doing? Discuss how sometimes when we go about doing tasks, we do not have our things together, and we end up spending a lot of time looking around for things. Describe a situation in which you tried to do something, but you did not have everything you needed before you started. What did you spend most of your time doing? What would have made the task get accomplished faster?

2. Was it easier or harder playing the game the way you did the second round?
   - What made it easier or harder? Discuss how it can often save time to put things away using a system. Remind the child how the monkeys were placed in sets according to color.
   - What are some things that you have trouble keeping up with?
   - What are some things that you could put away together so that next time you went to find them you would know where they are? Where can you put the things?

3. How was it playing the third round?
   - What was different?
   - Did having the monkeys in one place save time? Point out that when one begins a task it is critical to know what materials are needed. What materials were needed to play this game? Discuss how knowing where things are when you need them saves valuable time. Remember how difficult it was when you were looking all over the room for the monkeys compared to when they were all in one place? Relate this to how time can be saved doing tasks when one locates all the needed materials before starting a task.

Follow-Up Activity

Provide a copy of the "What do I Need?" worksheet (on the following page) for each student.

What Do I Need?

In each of the following scenarios, list the materials that would be needed for you to complete each task.

1. I have a spelling test to do.
    I will need:

    _____

    _____

2. I want to make a card for my sister's birthday.
    I will need:

    _____

    _____

3. I want to clean my room.
    I will need:

    _____

    _____

4. I want to finish my reading assignment at home.
    I will need:

    _____

    _____

Section 7: Respecting Others

Respect is a big word. Songs have been written about it, comedians joke about it, and everyone wants it. The problem is, so few people have not been taught how to give it. The games and activities in this section zero in on the complexity of respect. Society encourages children to "stand up for yourself", and "don't talk back to grown-ups", well what happens if the person they need to stand up to is a grown-up? It can be very confusing. Also, demonstrating how one's choice or behavior can directly affect someone else is difficult. Let's not forget how many children are not shown respect, yet we expect them to intrinsically know how to give it. All of these concepts are covered in this section.

A Respectful No

Objective

To teach one how to say no respectfully

Grades

1-8

Game

Jenga®

Participants work together to build the tower as high as possible. This game can be played with two – eight people.

Directions

1. Play according to the instructions included with the game. However, at random times during the game, look at the child and tell him/her not to get the block he/she has chosen to get from the tower.

2. Let the child know that you are going to tell him/her not to get the block. Teach the child to respond by looking you in the eye and stating, "I am going to choose this block." Afterwards, tell him/her to follow through with his/her plan.

3. Offer encouragement throughout the session.

Discussion

1. Let the child express feelings regarding saying no to others.
    *   How did you feel when you were to tell me "no" during the game?
    *   Did it get easier the more you did it? Discuss the answer and reinforce that saying no usually gets easier once one has continued practice. Discuss particular situations in the child's world where he/she has wanted to say no but did not. What happened?
    *   Who do you most often have trouble saying no to?
    *   Is there a way to say no and be respectful at the same time? Discuss.

2. Introduce the following skill steps as being a way to respectfully tell others no.
    Step 1. Look at the person.
    Step 2. Use a calm voice.
    Step 3. State clearly what you want or do not want.
    Step 4. Provide a reason for you response.
    *   Engage in a discussion about different ways of implementing these steps. Point out to the child the importance of voice tone, appropriate timing, and the difference between saying no and rebelling against authority. Describe times when saying no would simply be disrespectful. (Ex's. When parents give us instructions, when teachers give us instructions, etc.)
    *   When we were playing the game, what could you have done when telling me no that would have been disrespectful? (Ex.'s yelling "no," rolling his/her eyes when saying no, etc.)

Follow-Up Activity

Provide a copy of the "A Respectful No" worksheet (on the following page) for each student.

A Respectful No

In the following blanks, write the four skill steps.

>
>
>
>

Unscramble the words. Put an "X" on the words that definitely do no help one when saying no respectfully.

Word bank: eye contact, revenge, timing, scream, yell, practice, voice, patience, reason, calm, scream

oivec   yee   tncoact

_____   _____ _____

leyl   sorean

_____   _____

mintig   ractpiec

_____   _____

lcam   mescra

_____   _____

Domino Effect

Objective

To give a visual example of how one's choices or behaviors can affect others

Grades

K-8

Game

Jenga®

Participants work together to build the tower as high as possible. This game can be played with two – eight people.

Directions

1. Instruct the child to line the blocks up by standing the blocks on end.

2. Continue standing the blocks, one behind the other until all of the blocks are standing.
   a. As you are standing the blocks one behind the other, the blocks should be slightly off center.
   b. Feel free to make a particular design with the blocks if desired.

3. Once all the blocks are standing, gently tap the first block so that it will create a domino effect to knock all the other blocks down.

4. Repeat as many times as needed for the child to grasp the concept.

Domino Effect

Discussion

1. Before knocking the blocks down, ask the child what he/she thinks will happen when you push the block. Discuss how even though you did not touch the other blocks they fell over anyway. Give a hypothetical example of someone's choice or behavior effecting others ("Your class is lined up to go to lunch and someone runs into you and knocks you into the person behind you")

2. Ask the child to identify a time where a choice or behavior he/she made affected someone else. Talk about how if one considers the possible effect of his/her behavior before acting he/she can possibly reduce or eliminate the consequences of his/her behavior on someone else.

Follow-Up Activity

Provide a copy of the "Domino Effect" worksheet (on the following page) for each student.

Domino Effect

In the faces below, write the names of people in your family or at school to whom you can show respect to by thinking of the effect of your choices or behavior — FIRST!

Lean On Me

Objective

To assist one in considering the effects of one's behavior on others

Grades

K-8

Game

Pick Up Sticks

Participants try to remove sticks without moving the other sticks in the pile. This game can be played with two – eight people.

Directions

1. Review the rules of the game with the child.

2. Allow game to begin and continue until you and the child have had two-three turns.

3. Pause, and point out how some sticks are touching one or more sticks.

4. Praise the child when he or she carefully considers which stick to move, regardless if he/she is successful.

Discussion

1. Discuss how some of our decisions and/or behaviors appear to affect only us, but other times our decisions and/or behaviors seem to affect several people.

   - Ask the child to identify a situation where his/her behavior/decision affected other people. Who did the behavior/decision affect besides himself/herself?

   - If you were aware beforehand of the impact your behavior was going to have, would your behavior have been different? If so, how? Explain that one's decision/behavior may affect other people in positive ways or negative ways. Provide examples of each.

2. What are some ways that you can consider the possible effects of your behavior/decisions in the future? Provide scenarios of behaviors, and have the child identify the possible outcomes of the behaviors.

Follow-Up Activity

Provide a copy of the "Lean on Me" worksheet (on the following page) for each student.

Lean On Me

Draw a picture of yourself having a
positive affect on other people.

Objective

To define respect and to identify ways to show respect to others

Grades

K-8

Game

Mr. Potato Head Hot Potato Game®

Participants quickly toss the potato to each other before the music stops. This game can be played with two – eight people.

Directions

1. Play according to the instructions included with the game.

2. After playing a few rounds, engage students in a discussion. After defining respect, play the game by having each child verbally state and/or show a way he/she can respect others before throwing the potato to the next person. Children may need to be prompted initially. (ex's. of answers and/or things to do include: giving a compliment, throwing the potato gently, using an inside voice, telling someone they are doing a good job, helping someone, etc.)

3. Offer continual encouragement and feedback.

Respect?

Discussion

1. Discuss and define the concept of respect by answering the following questions. How do you show respect? Who do you show respect to?

   • Tell about a time you showed someone respect. Also, tell about a time someone showed you respect.

   • What are some ways to be disrespectful? Tell about a time someone was disrespectful to you. How did you feel? How did you respond?

   • Should you show respect to others even if they do not respect you? Explain your answer.

2. Think about some ways that you can show respect to others while playing this game. Introduce the new way to play according to direction #3.

Follow-Up Activity

Provide a copy of the "Respect?" worksheet (on the following page) for each student.

Respect?

In the following spaces, list at least one person you have trouble showing respect to.

⭐ _____

⭐ _____

⭐ _____

What can you do during the next week to show more respect to the person/people listed above?

The Buddy System

Objective

To emphasize the importance of respectful communication

Grades

2-8

Game

Guesstures®

Participants act out words in a limited amount of time. This game can be played with two – eight people.

Directions

1. Play according to the instructions included with the game.

2. Before beginning to play, use examples of words in the game to discuss how some possible clues may be hurtful if playing with certain people.

3. Play with teams of children who know each other.
   a. Discuss how some clues they may have chosen were not hurtful to their teammate because they had personal knowledge of that person, and probably know what could hurt their feelings, or trigger angry feelings in that person.

4. Mix the teams up, so that teammates have little or no personal knowledge of each other.
   a. Discuss how one may have felt more cautious about giving certain clues since he/she could not predict possible responses from his/her teammate due to lack of personal knowledge.

Discussion

1. How did you feel when you were paired with an acquaintance/friend versus someone you don't know very well?
   - Did you feel anxious, or worried that you might offend them in some way?
   - Who were you more concerned about possibly offending?

2. Did you give different clues to your friend? Identify others you are more likely to speak freely with. Identify people or situations where you are more likely to watch what you say.
   - Have you ever accidentally hurt someone's feelings by not thinking before speaking?
   - How did you feel in that situation?
   - What steps (if any) did you take to rectify the situation?

3. Describe a time when someone said something that hurt your feelings or triggered your anger.
   - How did you feel in that situation?
   - What steps (if any) did the other person take to rectify the situation?

Follow-Up Activity

Provide a copy of the "The Buddy System" worksheet (on the following page) for each student.

The Buddy System

I show others respect when I consider how they might feel before I do or say something.

Draw a comic strip illustrating yourself being respectful to others:

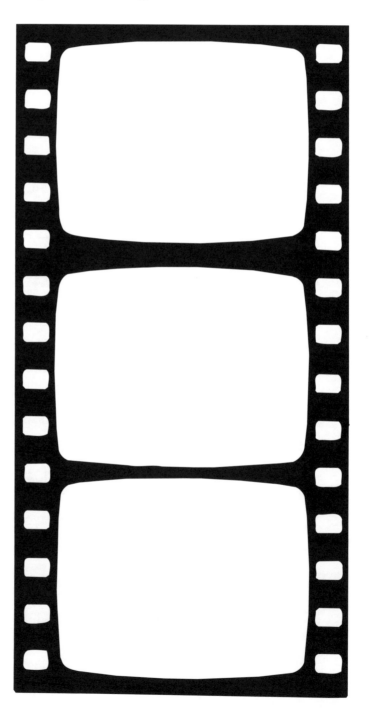

Section 8: Taking Responsibility

"Nobody takes responsibility anymore!" Have you ever heard this? Have you ever said this? Possibly: 'yes' to both. Learning to take responsibility for one's actions is a difficult life lesson. After all, who wants to say, "I did it, I messed up"? However, it is an essential part of character development. Before real change can occur, one must realize what he/she is currently doing is not working, and he/she needs to do something else. That realization involves taking responsibility, whether it is responsibility for choices or behavior, or both. It is a rather abstract lesson, which can make it challenging to explain to children. By using hands-on games, he/she can have a visual example of the importance of taking responsibility. It also provides an opportunity for the adult to model how to take responsibility.

Choice Can Equal Change

Objective

To introduce the concept that one is responsible for his or her choices and therefore, has the ability to make changes

Grades

K-8

Game

Don't Spill the Beans®

Participants try to stack as many beans as possible onto the bowl without making it tip over. This game can be played with two – four people per game.

Directions

1. First, play the game by giving the instructions that everyone will place their beans only on one side of the bowl. Do this several times, and each time count how many beans are placed on the bowl before it falls.

2. After a few rounds of play, give the instructions for all beans to be stacked on the other side of the bowl only. As rounds are played, again keep track with how many beans are placed upon the bowl before it falls.

3. Ask the child if there are any ways you all could be more successful at playing the game. (Make sure to point out that one could try to balance the beans on the bowl instead of putting them on one side.)

4. Play the game a few more rounds by placing the beans only on one side of the bowl.

5. Repeat direction # 3. Then repeat direction # 4. Continue this several times until you feel like the child will grasp the concept that for some thing to occur differently, one must make a choice to change and then follow through.

120

6. After discussion, play several rounds actually using the suggestions brainstormed for more effective play.

Discussion

1. How did you feel when we continued to play the game the same way over and over, even though we knew that was not the best way to play?
   - When we discussed ways we could play differently, did we come up with good ideas that might work?
   - Even though we came up with good ideas, did they really help us? Why not? (because we did not use them)
   - What would we have had to do in order for the ideas to have helped us? (we would have to change the way we played)
   - Whose decision was it to keep playing the same way? Who could have made the decision to play using the suggestions?

2. Point out how this is the same thing we do sometimes when we continue to make choices that produce negative results. We may have good ideas or know ways to do better, but we simply keep doing the same things. (Give an example of a time you continued to do something, but knew you would be more effective doing something differently). Reinforce that one must make the decision to change within himself/herself. No one can force you to change. You are responsible for your choices.
   - When you find yourself a pattern of behavior you want to change, what can you do to make a change?
   - Introduce the following skill steps:
     a. Recognize that you have the ability to change.
     b. Decide how or what you are going to change.
     c. Ask for help if you need it.
     d. Make the necessary changes.
        - Practice reciting the steps a few times.
        - Play the game according to direction #6 while applying the skill steps to the game process.

Follow-Up Activity

Provide a copy of the "Choice Can Equal Change" worksheet (on the following page) for each student.

Choice Can Equal Change

Answer the following questions.

1. Who has the ability to change? _____

2. Can anyone make you change? _____

3. What are the steps to change?

a.	b.
c.	d.

4. What is something you would like to work towards changing? _____

5. How can you use the skill steps to go about changing?

_____

_____

_____

_____

Does It Add Up?

Objective

To assist one in realizing how today's behaviors affect tomorrow

Grades

3-8

Game

Yahtzee®

Participants must add dice to have the highest score. This game can be played with two – eight people.

Directions

1. Play according to the instructions included with the game.

2. Remind the child during the game that if he or she fills in 2's with 4pts, and then he or she rolls 4 #2's (8pts), he or she cannot change his or her score.

3. As the game nears the end, point out the choice of waiting to Yahtzee or putting 0 in that blank.

4. Talk about your rationale for your choices as you play.

Does It Add Up?

...*Continued*

Discussion

1. Did you want to go back and change your score during the game?
   - What would you have done differently?
   - How did your choices affect your overall score? (Did you wait for a high roll which never came and then you had to put a 0 for your score? Did you put a 0 then Yahtzee or score a high roll for a number?)
   - Ask the child to identify a situation where a choice he or she made had an impact on a future choice or behavior.
   - What impact will the choices and your behavior have on you in the future?
   - What can you do to change this (if it is negative) or how can you maintain this (if it is positive)?

Follow-Up Activity

Provide a copy of the "Does It Add Up" worksheet (on the following page) for each student.

124

Does It Add Up?

In each situation, tell how that behavior will affect something in the future.

1. You followed all the instructions on a worksheet, and you did your best.

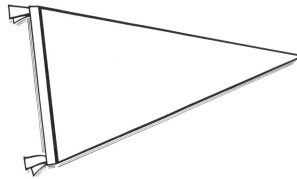

2. You decided to watch TV instead of cleaning your room.

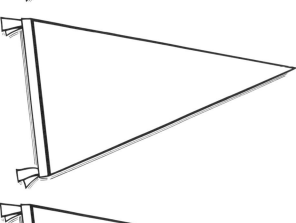

3. You cheated on a test during math.

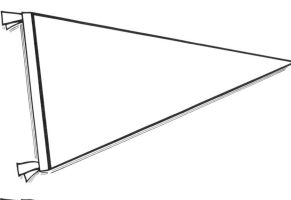

4. You stood up for someone who was being made fun of on the playground.

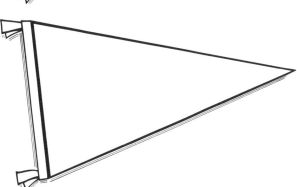

It's My Life

Objective

To assist in taking responsibility for choices

Grades

3-8

Game

Life®

Participants must choose different variables in "life," and the winner is the player who retires with the most money. This game can be played with two – eight people.

Directions

1. Play the game according to the instructions included with the game.

2. Play several times, changing the college/career option, as well as salary. *This game can be very lengthy and it may need to be spread over a few sessions. It can also be played in part such as changing the career and discussing the impact and not playing the entire game.

3. Each player must continue with the results of his/her choice, unless directed to change by the game.

Discussion

1. Did your "life" turn out the way you hoped?
    - Was it difficult to stick with your choices?
    - Which choices would you have liked to change after you started playing?

2. Review the choices you made and discuss the impact of your choices on your "life." Identify and discuss choices you have recently made that could have an impact on your future (for instance, if one has previously failed a subject and recently failed that same subject, they may not be able to pull that grade up and may possibly have to repeat that grade which could delay high school graduation. Another example would be the high school student who chose to take an advanced course that could count toward college credit). Encourage the child to take responsibility for his/her choices in the game and in real life.

Follow-Up Activity

Provide a copy of the "It's My Life" worksheet (on the following pages) for each student.

It's My Life

Copy this page or use other play money and distribute change to the child that equals $10.00 to use with the following activity page.

It's My Life

Your mom gives you $10.00 on Monday for your lunch money. You also need paper and a pencil, and you would like to buy snacks at recess. Use the table and decide how you will be responsible with your money?

Item	Price
Lunch	$1.50
Paper	$0.50
Pencil	$0.25
Chips	$0.50
Candy	$0.50
Soft Drink	$0.50

	Lunch	Paper	Pencil	Chips	Candy	Drink	TOTAL SPENT
Monday							
Tuesday							
Wednesday							
Thursday							
Friday							

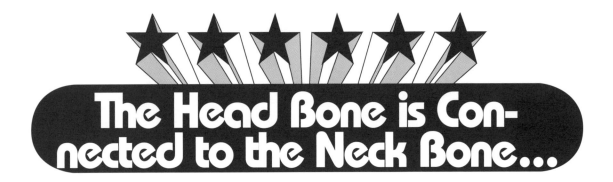

The Head Bone is Connected to the Neck Bone...

Objective

To assist one in becoming aware of the responsibility he/she has in taking care of his/her body

Grades

K-8

Game

Operation®

One uses tweezers to remove parts from the game board without touching the sides. This game can be played with two - eight players per game.

Directions

1. Review the rules of the game according to the instructions included with the game.

2. Before each player takes a turn, have him/her identify one thing he/she does or knows others do, that negatively effects the body part he/she is about to operate on (for example: smoking effects the lungs, drugs effects the brain and other parts, eating too much effects the stomach, not exercising could effect the arms and leg muscles, etc.).

3. Then ask each player to identify one positive thing he/she does or can do to have a positive affect on that body part (for example: eating more fruit

and vegetables is good for the muscles and brain, exercise regularly for strong bones and muscles, not smoking is good for the lungs, staying away from drugs is good for the brain, etc.).

4. After this, he/she can operate on the body part.

5. The game continues in this manner for each player until the entire operation is finished.

Discussion Topics

1. Who is responsible for your body? Emphasize that regardless of age, each person is ultimately responsible for his/her body

2. What are signs that let one know if he/she is being irresponsible with his/her body? (frequent illness, overweight, underweight, skin problems, body odor, etc.)

3. List ways that one will know that he/she is being responsible in taking care of his/her body (healthy, active lifestyle, good hygiene, etc.)

4. How do you think taking care of one's body impacts how one feels about himself/herself?

5. Identify at least one specific way you will take responsibility for your body this week.

Follow Up

Provide a copy of the "The Head Bone is Connected to the Neck Bone…" worksheet (on the following page) for each student.

The Head Bone is Connected to the Neck Bone...

In each box below draw a picture of yourself doing something healthy for your body.

You Owe Me!

Objective

To demonstrate the importance of being responsible

Grades

3-8

Game

Monopoly®

Participants try to collect the most property and money. This game can be played with two – eight people.

Directions

1. Play the game according to the instructions included with the game.

2. Emphasize that it is each player's responsibility to collect rent if another player lands on his/her property.
   *Due to the length of this game it can be spread out over 1-2 sessions.

You Owe Me!

...Continued

Discussion

1. Was it difficult to always be aware if another player landed on your property?
   - Why does the game have the rule that the property owner is responsible for collecting rent from other players when they land on his property?
   - As you obtained more properties, was it difficult to be responsible for each one? Process how you kept up with multiple properties.

2. Identify 1 or more responsibilities you have at home or at school. What makes you a responsible/irresponsible person in the areas you identified?
   - Identify other people you know who are responsible for you in some way (teacher is responsible for you while you are in his/her class, while the principal is responsible for the teachers and all the students, a police officer is responsible for the safety of the members of a community, your parent is responsible for the safety of you and your siblings, etc.)
   - What can you do to become more responsible?

Follow-Up Activity

Provide a copy of the "You Owe Me!" worksheet (on the following page) for each student.

You Owe Me!

Fill in the blanks by identifying things you are responsible for and then ask your teacher and/or parent(s) to grade you:

REPORT CARD		
I am Responsible for:	School	Home
1.		
2.		
3.		
4.		
5.		
6.		
7.		
8.		
9.		
10.		

Section 9:
Teamwork

What do a third grade class, baseball team, ballet class, school faculty and a family have in common? They are all examples of areas where people must work together as a team. It can be called many things: cooperation, working together, being a team player, but it all means the same thing – the ability to interact with others for a shared outcome. Teamwork is a skill that one uses all through life. It is critical to success in school, organized sports, higher education, and most occupations. However, many children do not naturally possess the ability to work well with others, so they must be taught. The games and activities in this section focus on demonstrating the importance of teamwork, and give opportunities for those who struggle with this skill to practice it in a safe environment.

Do You See What I See?

Objective

To assist one in developing the skills needed to work together with others as a team.

Grades

K-8

Game

Memory®

Participants try to find pairs of matching cards. This game can be played with at least 2, but no more than 6 people per game.

Directions

1. Prior to play, spread out the cards so that the players can familiarize themselves with the cards (you may also play with a few pairs of cards and not the whole deck).

2. While the players are looking at the cards that will be played, have them discuss identifying features of the cards and how one would describe each card. Find a common element, and emphasize it (for example: a picture of a strawberry would be "large, red strawberry") so that everyone playing is using the same or at least similar adjectives to describe each card.

3. Then, turn the cards over placing them in neat rows, and name the rows (for example: this is row 1, row 2, etc.) making sure each row has the same number of cards per row and the cards are aligned.

4. Each team should pick a player to describe the cards, and a player to chose the cards. The person who chooses the cards will close his/her eyes and tap two cards. The person who describes will turn the cards over, stating out loud the cards position (card A is in row 1 card 3, card B is in row 3 card 2) and then will describe each card as discussed earlier.

5. If a match is made, then that team gets another turn. If a match is not made, then the next team has a turn. The players who can look at the cards can tell their partner where a match is located (for example, Team 2 turns up a card previously seen, but did not make a match; it is Team 1's turn and the player who is describing the cards can say, "Go back to row 1 card 3 for the match to row 3 card 2.")

6. Play continues until all the matches are found.

7. Have the players switch roles.

Discussion Topics

1. Which role was more difficult—the role of the describer, or the chooser?
   - Ask players to discuss the pros and cons of their teammates job (do not allow personal attacks).
   - Ask players to offer advice to teammates for improvement in each role

2. Did you think that you and your partner made a good team? Why or why not?

3. Do you think this game would have been more difficult if we had not discussed how to describe the cards before playing? Explain.
   - Can you identify other times that communication either helped or hindered a team you were part of? (Remember, a team can be a class, a club, a family, or a group of friends.)
   - Brainstorm good communication skills (each person has knowledge of the topic, can be written or verbal, is not judgmental, is clear and concise, etc.)
   - Follow-up with a discussion of the importance of good communication skills when working with others

Follow Up

Provide a copy of the "Do You See What I See?" worksheet (on the following page) for each student.

Do You See What I See?

Decode the secret message by putting a line through the letters "x" and "z". Write the message on the lines provided.

```
x x x x x x x z x x x x x x g x x x z o x x x o z z z z d
t e x x x x x x x x a z z z z z m x x z z z z z z z z z z x
x x x x x s x x z x z x z z z z z z k z z z z n x x x x o
z x z x z x z w z x x x h z x z x z x z x z x z x z x
z o z x x x x x x x x x x x x x x x x x x x x x x w z z z z z
x z x z x z t z x z x z x z o x z x z x z x c x z x z x z o x z
x x x x x x x m x z x z x z m x z x z z z z z u z z z z
z z n x x x x x x x i x z x z x z c z x z x z x z a z z z z
z z z z z z z z z t x x x e . x x x x x x x x z z z z z z
```

_____

_____

_____

In the text boxes below, write statements that demonstrate good communication between team members.

In One Accord

Objective

To demonstrate the skill of working together to accomplish a task

Grades

2-8

Game

Jenga®

Participants work together to build the tower as high as possible. This game can be played with two – eight people.

Directions

1. Scatter the blocks onto the floor.
2. Discuss that the goal of the activity is for everyone to help in building an object, using good teamwork skills.
3. Tell the child/children to start. Observe what happens for a minute.
4. Ask them to stop, and introduce the following steps to aid in the process of teamwork.
   a. Come up with a plan that everyone agrees upon. (Decide what to build.)
   b. Assign jobs. (Who will build which part?)
   c. Do the jobs. (Actually build the object agreed upon.)
   d. Review work and make changes if necessary. (Did it turn out like everyone had planned, and do any changes need to be made?)

In One Accord

...*Continued*

5. Instruct the child/children to resume the game and implement the steps.

Discussion

1. What happened when I just told you to work together?
    - How did you feel?
    - How much got accomplished?

2. When playing using the steps, what was different?
    - Did you accomplish more or less?
    - How did you feel?
    - What would have happened if someone did not follow through with his/her part?
    - Have you ever been part of a team and someone did not do their part? Tell about it. How did you and other members of the team feel?
    - When someone is not doing his/her part on the team, what should you do?

Follow-Up Activity

Provide a copy of the "In One Accord" worksheet (on the following page) for each student.

In One Accord

Instruct the child to write in the skill steps, color/ decorate the scroll, and cut it out.

Following these steps will help a team accomplish a task:

1.

2.

3.

4.

It Takes Two

Objective

To emphasize the importance of learning to work well with others

Grades

K-8

Game

Jenga®

Participants work together to build the tower as high as possible. This game can be played with two – eight people.

Directions

1. Play the game according to the instructions included with the game.

2. Play a few rounds without any communication between players.

3. Play a few rounds with negative communication between players (moaning, bossing, blaming, etc.).

4. Play a few rounds with positive communication between players (suggestions, encouragement, etc.).

Discussion

1. What was it like to play the game without talking?
   Discuss advantages and disadvantages.
   - What was it like to talk while playing the game?
     Discuss advantages and disadvantages.
   - Which way of playing (positive/negative communication or no communication) produced the best results (which way was the tower the tallest)?
   - How did you feel when your teammates were negative with you?
   - How did you feel when your teammates were positive with you?

2. Identify an area in which you are part of a team (class, family, sport, club, group therapy, church, etc.).
   - What are the benefits of being part of a team? Are there disadvantages of being part of a team?
   - What type of a teammate are you (positive or negative)? List characteristics that you feel make you a good/bad teammate. List ways you can become a better teammate.

Follow-Up Activity

Provide a copy of the "It Takes Two" worksheet (on the following pages) for each student.

It Takes Two

List 3 characteristics of a good teammate:

1. _____

2. _____

3. _____

These are areas in which I am part of a team

It Takes Two

Copy the bookmark and allow the child to color and/or decorate it using the shapes.

I Am A Good Teammate!

Melting Pot

Objective

To demonstrate the benefits of teamwork

Grades

K-8

Game

Don't Spill the Beans®

Participants try to stack as many beans as possible onto the bowl without making it tip over. This game can be played with two – eight people.

Directions

1. Instruct the player(s) that the object of the game is to see how many beans can be placed on the pot without spilling the beans.
   *At this point, do not give directions for the players to work collaboratively.

2. After a few attempts, direct players to work together to get the most beans on the pot before it spills.

3. Set a predetermined goal of the number of beans on the pot and try to beat the goal each subsequent attempt.

Discussion

1. Were you more successful when you worked independently, or as a team? Discuss the effect that the placement of the beans has on the length of time before the pot spills.

   - Did you find your teammate's comments/suggestions helpful or annoying? Why?
   - Discuss characteristics of a good teammate.
   - Give an example of a situation where you had to cooperate with others in order to be successful

Follow-Up Activity

Provide a copy of the "Melting Pot" worksheet (on the following page) for each student.

Melting Pot

Find the words that characterize a good teammate.
The words can be backwards, up, down, or diagonal.

Supportive
Good sport
Encouraging
Teammate

Positive
Trust worthy
Focused
Teamwork

```
A G O O D S P O R T I W Q C M Z T
F F O I C Z E M O U L Y G C B A E R
O R T I V E V I T I S O P Q I M U U
C E J I J Z I M N E W G E M I P F S
U L I X E T I U E E T A M M A E T T
S E T L R O R T I O H I I E L W L W
E I Q R S V A L H J K M B N I O P O
D B V Y U M I K S D F N M P L J R R
J L D I M C Z X W T O I P M J K I T
O U A T E P Q L G S K A X V M Z R H
U E N C O U R A G I N G C Z P L L I Y
T I V S A K S U P P O R T I V E V Y I
```

Chose a word from the pot to fill in the blank.

This week, I will try to become a better teammate by
being more _____.

Mine + Yours = More

Objective

To demonstrate how working as a team can sometimes produce better results than working alone

Grades

2-8

Game

Boggle®

Participants try to find as many words as possible on the board during a three minute time period. This game can be played with two – eight people.

Directions

1. Play the game according to the instructions included with the game. Remember to set a score that will determine when there is a winner.

2. After playing 3 rounds keeping track of individual scores or after a winner is determined, discuss that everyone will now play as a team. Use the same score identified in the first rounds of play as the target score. At the end of the round, have the participants add their scores together.

3. Offer continual praise and feedback during the course of play.

Mine + Yours = More
...*Continued*

Discussion

1. When playing the game using individual scores, how long did it take someone to reach the target score?

    •   When playing as a team, how long did it take to reach that same score? Why did it take less time?

    •   Describe situations in which things are done better when people work as a team. Describe situations in which things may be done better when people work individually.

2. What are the advantages of being part of a team?

    •   Are there ever any disadvantages to being part of a team? If so, describe.

Follow-Up Activity

Provide a copy of the "Mine + Yours = More" worksheet (on the following page) for each student.

Mine + Yours = More

In the first two stars, write advantages to being part of a team. In the last star, draw a picture of yourself being part of a team.

Appendix

Descriptions of Games

1. **Ants in the Pants®**

   Participants try to make their ants jump into the pants by pressing the back of the ants.

2. **Barrel of Monkeys®**

   Participants try to form a chain using the monkeys.

3. **Battleship®**

   Participants try to sink an opponents ship by calling out coordinates.

4. **Bop-It®/Bop-It Extreme®**

   Participants quickly try to follow oral instructions given in the game.

5. **Boggle®**

   Participants try to find as many words as possible on the board during a three minute time period.

6. **Connect Four®**

   Participants try to connect four chips vertically, horizontally, or diagonally.

Descriptions of Games

...Continued

7. Don't Break the Ice®

Participants take turns knocking blocks of ice out of the game board while trying not to make the skater fall.

8. Don't Spill the Beans®

Participants try to stack as many beans as possible onto the bowl without making it tip over.

9. Guesstures®

Participants act out words in a given amount of time.

10. Guess Who®

Participants try to guess the character of the other person by asking investigative questions about the character.

11. Hangman®

Participants try to guess an opponents word. With each try that passes without a correct answer, the "man" gets a step nearer to being hanged.

12. Jenga®

Participants work together to build a tower using wooden blocks as high as possible.

156

13. Life®

Participants must choose different variables in "life," and the winner is the player who retires with the most money.

14. Memory®

Participants try to find matching pairs of cards.

15. Monopoly®

Participants try to collect the most property and money.

16. Mr. Potato Head Hot Potato Game®

Participants quickly toss the potato to each other before the music stops.

17. Operation®

Participants use tweezers to remove parts from the game board without touching the sides.

18. Perfection®

Participants try to place 25 shapes on the board within sixty seconds or less.

19. Pick-Up-Sticks

Participants try to remove a stick without moving any of the other sticks in the pile.

20. Simon®

Participants try to successfully repeat a pattern modeled by the game.

Descriptions of Games

...Continued

21. Taboo®

Teams provide verbal cues for a given word in a limited amount of time.

22. Twister®

Participants are given instructions to follow that involve putting their hands and feet on certain colored circles.

23. Yahtzee®

Participants must add dice to have the highest score.

References

Berg, B. (1989). The anger control game. Dayton, OH: Cognitive Counseling Resources.

Berg, B. (1990). The self-control game. Dayton, OH: Cognitive Counseling Resources.

Bettleheim, B. (1972). Play and education. School Review, 81, 1-13.

Crocker, J. & Wroblewski, M. (1975). Using recreational games in counseling. Personnel & Guidance Journal, 53(6), 453-458.

Friedberg, R. (1996). Cognitive-behavioral games and workbooks: Tips for school counselors. Elementary School Guidance & Counseling, 31(1), 11-20.

Kottman, T. (1990). Counseling middle school students: Techniques that work. Elementary School Guidance & Counseling, 25(2), 138-145.

Ants in the Pants©2004 Hasbro, Inc. Used with permission.

Barrel of Monkeys©2004 Hasbro, Inc. Used with permission.

Battleship©2004 Hasbro, Inc. Used with permission.

Bop-It©2004 Hasbro, Inc. Used with permission.

Bop-It Extreme©2004 Hasbro, Inc. Used with permission.

Boggle©2004 Hasbro, Inc. Used with permission.

Connect Four ©2004 Hasbro, Inc. Used with permission.

Don't Break the Ice ©2004 Hasbro, Inc. Used with permission.

Don't Spill the Beans©2004 Hasbro, Inc. Used with permission.

Guesstures ©2004 Hasbro, Inc. Used with permission.

Guess Who©2004 Hasbro, Inc. Used with permission.

Jenga/Jenga Extreme©2004 Hasbro, Inc. Used with permission.

Life©2004 Hasbro, Inc. Used with permission.

Memory©2004 Hasbro, Inc. Used with permission.

Monopoly©2004 Hasbro, Inc. Used with permission.

Mr. Potato Head Hot Potato Game©2004 Hasbro, Inc. Used with permission.

Operation©2004 Hasbro, Inc. Used with permission.

Perfection©2004 Hasbro, Inc. Used with permission.

Risk©2004 Hasbro, Inc. Used with permission.

Simon©2004 Hasbro, Inc. Used with permission.

Taboo©2004 Hasbro, Inc. Used with permission.

Twister©2004 Hasbro, Inc. Used with permission.

Yahtzee©2004 Hasbro, Inc. Used with permission.

Notes